Prompts!

Recent Titles by 39 West Press

Striking the Black Snake: Poems from Standing Rock
MG Salazar

A Secret History of the Nighttime World
Jason Ryberg

Black Girl Shattered
Sheri Purpose Hall

Novel Cliché: Aphorisms
Jeanette Powers

Corazón y una lengua peregrina
Latino Writers Collective

Ghost Sign
Al Ortolani, Melissa Fite Johnson, Adam Jameson, JT Knoll

Nomadic? Rover by Day Singing These Gang Plank Songs of the Ambler
Hugh Merrill

Gender Treason
Ryan Wilks

Tiny Chasm
Jeanette Powers

Undiscovered Paladins: Westward Rhymes Revisited
j.d.tulloch

Fringes
Ricardo Quinones

Prompts!

A Spontaneous Anthology

edited by
jeanette powers & j.d. tulloch

39 WEST PRESS

39 WEST PRESS
Kansas City, MO
www.39WestPress.com

39 WEST
Ⓟ Ⓡ Ⓔ Ⓢ Ⓢ

Copyright © 2016 by 39 West Press

All rights reserved. No part of this book may be reproduced, scanned, or distributed in any printed or electronic form, including information storage and retrieval systems, without permission. Please do not participate in or encourage piracy of copyrighted materials in violation of the author's rights. Please purchase only authorized editions.

First Edition: October 2016

ISBN: 978-0-9908649-7-4

Library of Congress Control Number: 2016953067

This book is a work of fiction. Names, characters, places, dates, and incidents are products of the author's imagination, or are used fictitiously, satirically, or as parody. Any resemblance to actual persons, living or dead, business establishments, events, or locales is entirely coincidental.

10 9 8 7 6 5 4 3 2

Design & Layout: Jeanette Powers & j.d.tulloch
Front Cover Art: Ryan Wilks (wilkspainting.com)
Back Cover Art: Kathryne Husk

39WP-14

To the open mic poets of the Uptown Arts Bar's Poetic Underground

Special thanks to Ryan Wilks for creating the amazing cover art based upon the following prompt: double takes and belly aches

contents

introduction
ORIGINS OF *PROMPTS! A SPONTANEOUS ANTHOLOGY*   1

zophia mcdougal aka "petunia meat"
DRAINED: A LETTER FROM YOUR CAN OPENER   5

mark matzeder
MAJIK MIRROR'S REFLECTION   9

william edmond dozier
DO LAWNMOWERS DREAM OV TALL GRASS?   10

mendy shakti
GHOSTS OF ECHOES   12

jason preu
LITTLE ROBIN REDBREAST DECIDES TO CLIP HER WINGS   13

hanna doss
PLAID GOES SOLID   15

kathryne husk
YOU POISONED THE WATER   17

beth gulley
SAINT SWAN   19

matt keck
THEY SAY NOTHING RHYMES WITH PURPLE   20

jeanette powers
NON-OBJECTIVE PORTRAIT OF KARMA   21

$adgirl
THE INVISIBLE MAN GETS A PRESENT   24

hugh merrill
IN TEARS   26

michael wray
SWAN DIVES & CIGARETTES   27

alisha escobedo
GROUNDED AIRPLANES   28

lindsey martin-bowen
MESSAGES FROM MY SHOWER   29

victor clevenger
SHE   31

danielle corcione
MOVING DAY BLUES   33

maci branch
A FELLOWSHIP OF FOUND ART   34

jane blakely
FALLOW FIELDS   37

jen appell
A GALE FORCE WHISPER   38

josé faus
EARLY BIRD AND SOUR GRAPES   39

ezhno martin
GOIN' HOME   42

paul koniecki
TAMING OF THE SCREW   44

amber rentfro
AFTER DARK DIRECTIONS   46

kira burton
#RELATIONSHIPGOALS   48

abraham nathenson
TAKING CARE OF MY PET ANCHOR   50

shawn neustadt
ABSOLUTE FUTILITY   51

fredric sims
A LONELY BOOK   53

jen harris
POETRY IS   55

chico sierra
THE LINE IN THE SAND   57

shawn pavey
HOLLOW POINT   58

eve ott
MY GARDEN HOSE   60

tara quirk
HOPSCOTCH WITH MARSUPIALS   61

paul rola
CHANCE MEETING   62

james benger
LITERALLY HOW IT HAPPENED … FIGURATIVELY SPEAKING   63

roy beckemeyer
THE PRODIGAL SON GOES TO THE DISCO   64

jason ryberg
UNCLE MIKEY'S SUNDAY MORNING GITTY-UP-AND-GO-GO JUICE   65

andrea caspari
Lovely — 66

sara minges
Barbie's Mishap in High Heels — 67

dc lozano
A Small Bite in the Right Place — 68

lauren schrader
The Infiltration of Imperialism — 69

claire verbeck
[In Relation To:] — 71

ashley bellinghausen
Student of Sour Miso Soup — 72

matt butler
Famous Coffee Shops are for Boring People — 73

eileen victoria schroeder
The Little Scarecrow — 74

kathryne husk
Infantilized to Death — 77

brandon whitehead
Things Not to Do (Unless You are Dead) — 78

joel l. archer
Armadas — 80

sheri hall
#LaughingWhileBlack — 81

nathan thomas
Two Inches Deep — 82

edgar mason
Ping Pong and King Kong   83

sid yiddish
Bring Out the Dead ©   84

huascar medina
Prayer for an Atheist or an Email Marked for Spam   85

greta moore
Pouring Salt   86

m'vyonne payne
Spring with Stockholm Syndrome   87

j.d.tulloch
Chalklines in Effigy   88

jeanette powers
Unused Prompts   90

introduction
ORIGINS OF *PROMPTS! A SPONTANEOUS ANTHOLOGY*

Poetic Underground—a whiskey drinking, verbal slinging, raucous and righteous open mic poetry sequence—has been going strong at the Uptown Arts Bar in Kansas City, Missouri since 2012. The weekly event draws a rich diversity of dedicated versifiers, from cherry-popped first poem poets to tear-jerker slam giants, tight construction academic poets, and the grist of the grind small press poets. Every level of poetry can be witnessed (and heard) at open mic night.

Prior to *ghosting*—when a Guest Host leads the Poetic Underground festivities on the bonus, fifth Wednesday of a month—in June 2016, Jeanette Powers sent out a social media call egging on the open mic poets to contact her and request a prompt: a short, personally crafted phrase intended to be the inspiration for NEW SHIT! to spit at open mic night. *New Shit!* is what the audience shouts when a poet takes the stage to perform new material. In fact, a lot of community shouting occurs at Poetic Underground: *Speak Poet!*, *Rewind!*, *ULIT!*, and *Listen to the Poem!*

By open mic night, Jeanette had issued over one-hundred prompts, which led to the epic readings of volumes of New Shit! But other folks, many of whom were unable to attend open mic, wanted to be part of the shenanigans. So, the idea of a prompts book was born. And to expand its reach, she disseminated prompts beyond the open mic community to artists and scriveners across the land.

This spontaneous anthology represents the outpouring of new work by both fledgling and established writers and artists, which was engendered, simply, by the offer of a prompt.

The poems are presented here with minimal editorial revisions and appear, mostly, as each respective author submitted them. A list of unused prompts can be found at the end of this book. Please appropriate these gems to craft your own poems!

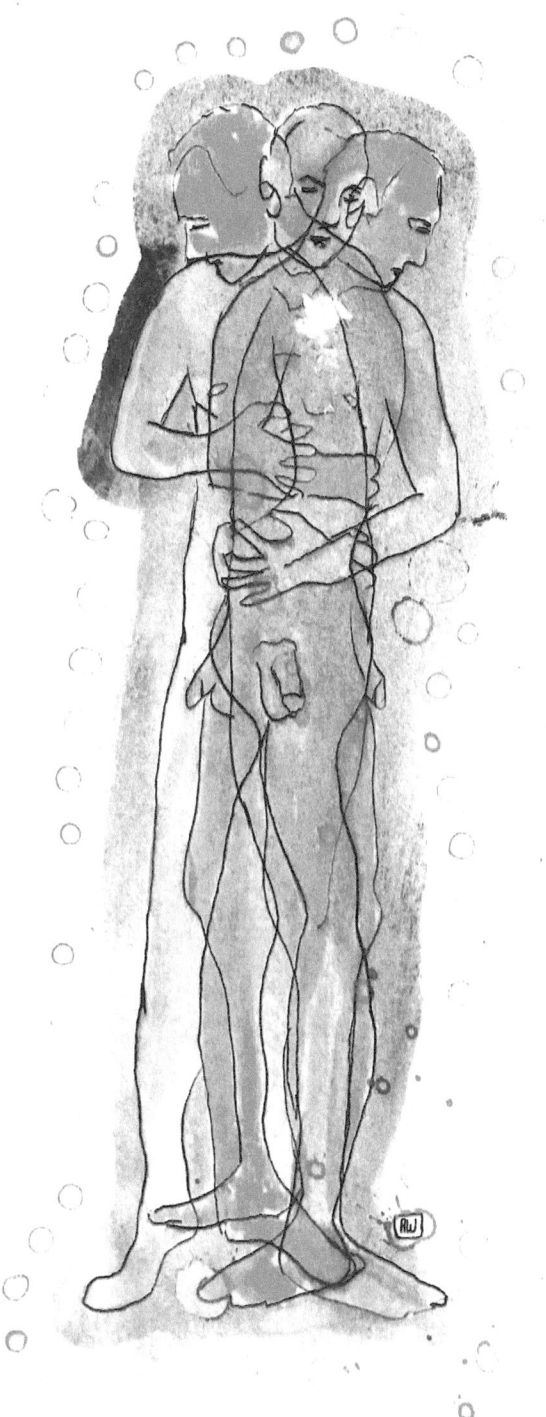

zophia mcdougal aka "petunia meat"
DRAINED: A LETTER FROM YOUR CAN OPENER

They

want me dead (echoes "and me" signaled by me raising my hand).
They want me dead, and I don't even know their name.
Could the whole world
take one deep breath at the exact same time? Maybe even two?

Are they willing to die for this?
Are we willing to die for this?
Our will to die?

                                          draining!

Trying to talk about anything that won't bring up hate right now.
The sky is fucking blue.
They have robot clones which they will use to become superstars.
If you're not in love, I will stop falling.
My name is, I am
My name is, I am
My name is, I am

                                          draining!

My pronouns are crying out to the hand
squeezing my limbs and my teeth crave aluminum
as each bite serrates through beatdowns and disgust.

They are there, but
they get the initial pour

                                          draining!

I'm telling you
wings are the real thing

and magic dust exists because
this blade serrating titanium
gets help from somewhere.

                                          draining!

They
want me dead   (echoes "and me" via hand motion)

tiny secretions
so small that love is getting confused, as
pride arrives its insides in order to belt out

"Hey! We deserve ourselves too!"

                                          draining!

I'm so sorry
everything isn't fine
if I were in your shoes
I'd slice never-ending circles
in the name of salt.

                                          draining!

Someone will warn them,
"be careful, you're gonna get arthritis."
Then they will keep going on their merry way
with intention and representation
similar to the curtain in your window.

                                          draining!

Warning, I do not run out of breath
I am a machine
acting on the behalf of the people of chaotic
existence.
I am opening cans

of non linear whoop ass
in order for your 90 degree angles to think otherwise.

I am draining rainbows
from containers holding tough love
which seems to be an afterthought lately.
And natural sunlight into your
liver, soaking up the word disease.

They want me dead.
                        (echoes "and me" via hand motion)

We are a thing
from a thing
raised in a thing
believing a thing
that the thing itself can't prove

                      draining!

without creating a thing
for the thing that shows
the things ability to move

                      draining!

and all of the other things
are getting mad and confused

                      draining!

while the people of imaginary things
feel beat up and used

                      draining!

all the things are fighting now
and they are on their last leg

they are more capable of standing off
rather than being a thing together, on a bed.

draining!

It seems as though the things can't talk right now,
they've all been cutting into more than they know how
their structure is different from then, it's now …

draining!

the thing is
the thing's thing.

Drained.

prompt: a letter from your can opener
microbio: come to dinner on sunday! (ig: @zophiamcdougal).

mark matzeder
MAJIK MIRROR'S REFLECTION

We had a wily night of sorcery
In which a wily knight fulfilled his vow
And bowed before the Sorceress' feet
Pledged Fealty and all he had endowed
Her with, though Life withheld and hid away
Against the day he might require escape
Pandora's box of tricks came into play
His machinations wove a stealthy cape.

For spells are words and poems are spells unsighed
Not wed to Reality but spinning
Tapestries of Dreams we wipe from our eyes
As Dawn liberates our day's beginning.

Merrily down the stream to the well
Awake in the dream and fresh out of spells.

prompt: wily night of sorcery
microbio: low-level spellcaster & consummate rogue.

william edmond dozier
Do Lawnmowers Dream ov Tall Grass?

Do androids dream ov electric sheep?
Can tigers live as the goat?
Could the lawnmower love the grass?

Humans n Our hubris,
whine We r better & above all else,
divine & not dust.

"Only We have consciousness & intelligence!",
many small minds scream,
"Only We may love!"

Like magic, magnetism attracts opposites,
alike yet not the same,
with or w/o a brain.

Machine like Man must love
the smell cut grass screams,
even as We hurt it.

Green leaf volatiles signal distress
as its blades slice through,
revealing a twisted, 1sided love.

Left alone outside or n a garage,
waiting, yearning 2 do its 1 will,
torture what he has come 2 love.

Up & down, back & forth,
over & over again it runs
with the grass tickling its undercarriage.

Outside under the Sun, free!
Then hidden away, yet again?

Once more he yearns, 4 her.

The mower would if it could
dream ov tall green grass, lawns
needing its love w/o even knowing.

If the lawnmower could love the grass,
caring 4 his love, might Man then
nurture & not annihilate nature all love?

prompt: the lawnmower falls in love with the grass
microbio: painter, philosopher, wordsmith, eremite & 1-armed dead man.

mendy shakti
GHOSTS OF ECHOES

Haunted or enchanted?
Exclaimed then pranced and panted
tired from the summer sun
what was once proclaimed
will eventually come undone
so we call to the shallows
of our skulls as we dream
alive with vibrance and color
unlike any seen on a screen
wavelengths that sink and carve
weaving with howling hoots
got these dreamed up saplings
shaking to their roots as sound
throbs through the stone walls
of time and enters
one more sleeping mind:
to express the awakening screech
from these ghosts of echoes unseen.

prompt: ghosts of echoes
microbio: sustainability enthusiast, holistic thinker, grateful to express.

jason preu
Little Robin Redbreast Decides to Clip Her Wings

In many ways, Little Robin Redbreast
     was a lot like you and me:

          late-night, half-drunk, listening
          to Taylor Swift and singing,
          "In Wonderland, we both went mad ..."
          She was a lot like you and me,
          'cept she was a bird
          and birds can fly
          and humans can't fly
          and birds can't cry
          sooooo ...

Little Robin Redbreast
decides to clip her wings;
snippy snappy goes her scissors,
now she hops while she sings.

Little Robin Redbreast
comes to visit me;
this is what she whistles,
"Don't you like what you see?"

But along comes wittle Pussy-Cat,
and a'shivering goes she;
Little Robin Redbreast
stares up at tall, dark trees.
Yes, around comes wittle Pussy,
away Robin tries to run;
sings little Robin Redbreast —
"My god, what have I done?"

Little Robin Redbreast
hops to a seaside cliff;

Pussy-Cat slinks after her,
sandpaper tongues his kitty lips.

Little Robin chirps and cries,
and what does Pussy say?
"You've cut yourself off from the sky
and now I'll have my way."

Pussy-Cat then leaps to kill
the flightless little bird;
grounded by an unknown will,
sad melodies unheard.

prompt: little robin redbreast decides to clip her wings
microbio: jason's bio wants you to fly, fly, forever fly.

hannah doss
PLAID GOES SOLID

My skirts had to be knee length.
Good girls are modest.
The plaid pattern blurred the lines between girl and woman.

I wasn't in Catholic school, but close enough for the story.
The brothers and sisters of our home church took turns
teaching us the valuable lessons of life.

My eleven-year-old self was disgusted at the way the other girls
talked about our male classmates. Their butts, their packages.
I heard no respect or dignity coming from their freshly glossed
lips. I watched in horror as they drooled over the young flesh
that ran around the playground, and it made me cringe.

Treat others as you would want to be treated.
Wasn't that something that was drilled into our heads daily?
We are all human after all.

I decided I was above it and kept to my journal.

I found that old journal entry while I was packing up my life
the other day and it made me cry.

Decades later the skirts are mid-thigh length.
Being modest is pointless.
People only see what they want to look for.
Solid black makes me feel safer.
It hides the years of abuse my body has experienced.
The belly of motherhood.
The teeter totter has tilted, and it has left me in the dirt.

I've learned many lessons on and off the playground since then.
My sympathy for those young boys comes from a different place.
The feeling of being an object is one that I can now identify with.

I still am disgusted with the way my playmates treat one another.
These days I find myself hiding more than seeking.

Afraid of the bullies that want to flex their stupidity.

Tag is only fun when everyone wants to play,
and the boundaries of home are kept safe.

Plaid.
Solid.
Polka-dotted.
Long.
Short.

The skirt makes no difference.

What's under the skirt makes no difference.

Realizing that we are all human, and we all deserve respect and love ...

That is the only thing that will ever make a difference.

I still keep to my journal,
if only to remind myself to voice the obvious.

prompt: plaid goes solid
microbio: human. mother. passionate.

kathryne husk
YOU POISONED THE WATER

you poisoned the water
with blue sticky threats
chiding me for being unable to breathe
hide quoted text
through salty chapped lips
from fingers pressing silent
hoping i would drown

instead, i knit myself
a tank of briny air
to breathe in your ocean

and you scoffed
that my accommodation
makes me freakishly deviant
from the other mermaids
and is why i'm beneath you
i'm not allowed to make waves in your sea

my fins were weak
so i fashioned new ones
from good intentions
and academic definitions
though it was a clumsily graceless glide
i could swim with the rest of you

but, with soggy desecrations
you mocked me for my finless life
you poisoned the water
with blue sticky threats
chiding me for being unable to see
through the muck and filth that you left
in your wake

so i made myself goggles
with glass from the holy sea
that tumbled and dove
until its edges were worn
politically smooth
and correctly even

you tell me i trouble your water
because i still can't see like you

i bound this aid to my body
to function in your sea
i can breathe
and see
and glide
so you shame me
by calling me human
but i'm still a fucking mermaid

prompt: mermaids with scuba gear
microbio: artist. poet. activist.

beth gulley
Saint Swan

A quick Google search
for the ugly duckling
meets Pygmalion's wife
yields no masterpiece
to inspire ekphrastic poetry.

Instead a tiny
blue meme
pops up.

Wait, I'm still thinking!

And there it is,
the essential
difference between
a live cygnet
and a marble
statue.

The living animal,
misnamed, grows up
outside its own culture.
And the perfect object,
cold and flawless,
has no brain.
While both represent
the make-over story,
I'd take the duckling
for my patron saint.

prompt: the ugly duckling meets pygmalian's wife
microbio: drinking too much coffee in paola, kansas.

matt keck
They Say Nothing Rhymes with Purple

and who are we
to argue?
Just a drop, a drip, half a damn drop, really,
making non-existent ripples
in this vast prismatic smut
blinding ourselves to the light
as we are
one, two, three shakes away.
Casting shade,
what shade? A shade of pink, of gray —
another shade of gray so mommy can plop
her fat ass on the dryer and shake the afternoon away
when you can't see what's new, or perceive
the way your eyes were meant to.
You add new slants, new angles, new ways to break
that you could never comprehend
without shaking the form to begin with,
Nothing rhymes with purple?
That's hurtful.
Dayyyyyum girl, you got a shirt full!
Ok, whoa, whoa, I'm sorry, whoa.
I'm just shaking out these daddy issues
with a bottle booze and a bottle of paint
fuck the brand, whatever's cheapest.
I'll make my splash
in this vast canvas
of fear and fighting and fucking
I am just a drip of purple
a drop of royal bullshit.

prompt: what rhymes with purple
microbio: a standup comic & a real motherfucker.

jeanette powers
NON-OBJECTIVE PORTRAIT OF KARMA

You accessorize like a berzerker in a party store
you leap to spider ring, bangle bracelet, cubic tiara, sci-fi anklet
a chain and lock necklace you don't have keys for
you are frantic as a cat scared up a tree by a feral dog
you buy a cleopatra armband of actual spitting cobras
a first aid kit for a purse, your manicure stays stubbornly perfect
you fetchingly model yet another hot or stable or big-dicked
disposable relationship and most recently, a real novelty:
                              a puppy.
I mean a real 5-star-god-damn-movie-dog
with a heart shaped spot, one ear that sticks up, 3 legs and a hop.

A thousand husked oysters are wagging their meaty tongues
at your feet for the honor of being pearls at your throat.
You string yourself up with the charisma of a blood bath.
Your red rosacea cheeks and varicose purple turkey neck
have more layers of bases and foundations and powders
than lashes on a very misbehaved slave's back:
you cover your tracks with such panache.

Even your entire bellicose fortress is an adornment
and tribute to coping with your generous generalized anxiety.
The carefully placed every-last-detail-exactly-where-it-must-be
designed to generate safe directed and easy conversations
about the obvious impossibility of anything not being just right.

Every painting is level with righteous justice and impunity
the floors are waxed with the panicked fury of tragedy
there's no longer a bit of plaque in a single spot of grout or tile.
Clean as a whistle, you say, more often than not.
The shedding dog is directed to be neatly asleep in the kennel,
though we hear him whine a protest at the door.
Secretly, you fashion fine linens and shit where you sleep.
But at dinner, everyone laughs with you while you dwell

on your unique set of traumas and on the quirky cute sickness
and slickness between your trim head and your smart thighs.

But your sapphire obsidian crown jewel, the pièce de ré·sis·tance
the singular signature totem we all kowtow at the bottom of
is the prismatic and uncuttable obelisk of your steadfast illness.
You wear the lazily draped, whining and habitual incantation
of a chronic aching migraine headspace like a suffocating caul
hand embroidered with a patterned chattering groan
to generate the obligatory and helpful reactions of your guests
the necessary, endless attention, gentle condolences
the constancy of leaping to your rescue
you damsel, you Rapunzel, you sleeping beauty
you are the protagonist of every episode
in classic soap-opera, haute drame style.

Princess-baby-girl sends the butler to shut that incessant barking up.
The bell ring of your displaced disdain chimes against
the silver tea service and luminous chandelier as you sing out
I just don't know ever why I keep sabotaging myself
and nervously spin the ruby rings and clanking bangles
from wrist to elbow and all twitter and giggle and gangle
while tossing back mounds of perfectly conditioned hair.
The dog's yap yapping is giving away the chaos that hides under.
Your heart is racing with all this exposure.

(I won't mention your accessory of choice, darling.)

But do lift high that Waterford chalice of vintage sweet port
and toast to high time for new curtains, wallpaper and chairs,
a whole new look, a brand new, a something different, in fact.
Why hasn't that dog gone and just shut up!
You paint yourself into a corner with such pride.
Hire yourself a new interior decorator to dress your insides
in the latest craze and diagnose your mind with the newest trend
in therapist wet dreams. Surround yourself with the most
desirable passing fashion, investigate the whim of the scene
have them paint the mirrors with what you'd like to see there.

Have them paint your excuses as if they were reasons
and hand paint them as aphorisms with a folksy wooden frame.

The puppy keeps baying a warning in the background.
Your prom dress and seat cushions are torn by his baby teeth.
You keep him in the garage. You stake him in the backyard.
For so many years to come, when he sees you he bares his teeth.

Well, it's true that you get the dog you deserve.

prompt *(given by shawn neustadt)*: non-objective portrait of karma
microbio: mirrors are tricky; i love you, margaret.

$adgirl
THE INVISIBLE MAN GETS A PRESENT

He was made from something else.
Cut from glass.
Muscles.
Hard against my skin.
Face pressed against mine.
But I could see.
Right through him.
When I told him.
That I value transparency.
He stabbed me in the front.
I may not have seen him fuck her.
But then.
I never saw him fuck me either.
Saran-wrap centerfold.
And I'd been seeing him.
For years.
He wore a cheesy sports hat.
Always falling off.
And materializing in public.
He told me looks didn't matter to him.
But the invisible man.
Is vain.
As fuck.
And I've never known a man.
To spend so long.
In his own reflection.
Ghost hands feel like my father's.
All knotted muscle and finger hair.
And I thought I was broken before.
Conveniently absent.
Selective vision.
Despite never knowing their color.
I still managed to get lost in those eyes.
Sometimes.

What you don't see hurts the most.
For a glass man.
He sure knew how.
To shatter me.
So when his special day came around.
Again.
There was only one thing.
I could give.
To the invisible man.
An invisible me.
And mark my words.
I'm never.
Looking.
Back.

prompt: the invisible man gets a present
microbio: $uicide gang. do the right thing. (thesadgirl.com).

hugh merrill
In Tears

in tears of remembrance the land of dreams begins
my souls are carried by twilight's sky
forming clouds of what seemed to have been mine
now all changed and gone

the wind dries your saltwater tears
before they can soothe my thirst
the rain does not reach the desert floor
here all remains dry and dead
shouting in different languages we cannot speak

grim reaper of this sunset memory
leaving all of us in solitude, alone
end the end to become one
within the nocturnal cycle of mourning and becoming.

prompt: salt water won't soothe your thirst
microbio: born, raised southern, broken family, escaped to art school/poetry.

michael wray
SWAN DIVES & CIGARETTES

Inhale, exhale … shit, pack's empty.
Brother, can I get a cigarette?
Sister, can I get a light?
Eyes, empty, search for redemption.

Today, I will fall to the floor
a jeering crowd will cry out for blood
will have me cry tears of red
as I get back up.

The fix is in, you know, and so do they.
But the spectacle still tantalizes.
I fall once, twice, a third time.
My blood spattered across the ring.

This time, I stay down, wait for 10.
I could have gotten up, but the crowd …
that's not what they came to see.
They wanted a perfect swan dive, and I obliged.

You ask what you can do for this battered warrior
broken and bloody after his clown act? Well …
Brother, can I get a cigarette?
Sister, can I get a light?

prompt: swan dives & cigarettes
microbio: aspiring person.

alisha escobedo
GROUNDED AIRPLANES

prompt: grounded airplanes
microbio: egotistical & selfless & sometimes makes decent art.

lindsey martin-bowen
MESSAGES FROM MY SHOWER

Overnight, they appear—
almost invisible—watery
hieroglyphics running
in rivulets through steam
creeping across glass.

My bones cling to my skin
when I try to decipher
these arcane messages.

Then, a voice like pipes hissing
sends me to a sea
in Galilee, silver
as the handhold I grab.

I am Jephthah's daughter—
it sings.

> My only sin
> is greeting Father when he
> returns from battle.
>
> I dance and play a tambourine.
>
> But he vowed to sacrifice
> the first one he sees.
>
> That person is me.
>
> So I ask two months
> to mourn my virginity:
> a life without issue,
> a woman failed.

Later, I read Israelite
women still trek
a pilgrimage to mourn her
four days each year.*

I wonder where her bones lie
and why she had to die.

See Judges 11: 30-40.

prompt: messages from my shower
microbio: *crossing kansas with jim morrison* is her sixth published book.

victor clevenger
SHE

has
twenty-seven
bones

forward
from her wrist

to make a fist
when
she's pissed

or to grasp my
neck when
we kiss.

lips split
lips rip
hips sway

put away
put away
put away

the blade

when
my back
is against the wall

five feet
six inches
tall

with tens
of thousands
of circulatory
miles inside
of my skin

i have never
forgotten the
time in the
shower when she
brandished her
razor & told
me

it only takes
one good
slice
perfectly placed
to put you
on a cold slab
with a tag
on your toe
motherfucker

prompt: dissection of anatomy
microbio: best friend boa's will still sink a tooth in you.

danielle corcione
Moving Day Blues

cardboard boxes
piled to
the ceiling
unorganized
 yet
still labeled
by room

this is
our third
rental van
this year
and
it's
only
May

prompt: moving day blues
microbio: freelance writer based in omaha.

maci branch
A Fellowship of Found Art

A fellowship of lost art
Sitting quietly on dusty shelf
Find your way into my heart
Teach me how to be myself
Your panels illuminate beautiful pages
Pictures and Portraits oh so pure
That recycles the monomyth throughout the ages
The labors of heroes to endure
Yonder in local comic book tavern
A fellowship just waiting to be found
Dive into that deep dark cavern
Underneath the mighty ground
Oh fellowship of found art
Let your way into my heart
Mold me with your words
Lose me in your sea of stories
Sing your songs like yonder birds
Amaze us with your daring glories
Get issues one through one hundred
The sweetest of fruits
To be scavenged and hunted
Yes I am Groot
And you are too
So we tear into our findings
To know what is true
Unlocking the bindings
The river story flows away
Molding us like hands with clay
Get us through oh dark knight
Bring the dawn of yellow sun
New gods we be in all our might
Just stop the jester and his fun
Weave a web across tall buildings
Go to school to learn your powers

Lift Mjolnir, thunder wielding
Avengers Assemble in yonder towers
Preachers that make cigs look cool
A family of ducks and their relations
Drunken exorcists on bar stools
And Amazons who know elation
To tie in bonds an ill-spent youth
With that golden rope of truth
All this and more
In long white boxes
At that magical store
I burrow like foxes
Book after most lonesome book
Of Faustian bargains, and wicked deeds
Yet onwards and backwards I must look
So that I may plow my seeds
And you may say this is only for boys
Quiz me with trivia so I can prove
That all the gold spent on books and toys
Is my real and genuine groove
Even when you see this is me
Don't assume this means we
Identity, this means I
Before you were here
Free to fly in the sky
Not caring about jealous peers
Competition this is not
Yet you complain this is all the same
Instead of just enjoying the plot
Casting shade this is not tame
Trivializing my passion, my love
Just like the trivia that shows your best
So you know the identities of Hawk and Dove
I don't care, just give it a rest
Not from you a single sound
Not when a fellowship of art is to be found
I'm not here to prove a point
Not to be angered and shook

I just want to smoke a joint
And take a peep inside this book
See the judge of Mega-City One
Here Frankie boy let loose a shot
Blasting punishment from their guns
While A man with no fear senses a lot
These are for me
As I struggle and grow
So take it from me
I don't care what you know
This is my garden my child my heart
My precious fellowship of found art

prompt: a fellowship of found art
microbio: from catholic school babe to queer bodied goddess.

jane blakely
Fallow Fields

There are no fallow yards
in my neighborhood — even when we try
to let the lawns just be,
we realize quickly
that brown grass is unacceptable.

prompt: fallow fields
microbio: runs every day but can't skip rocks.

jen appell
A GALE FORCE WHISPER

prompt: a gale force whisper
microbio: mother. musician. singer/songwriter. photographer. nature enthusiast.

josé faus
EARLY BIRD AND SOUR GRAPES

Lost in the dung pile
a fox waxes on about capital
Is it them he asks
as if with one snort
all the ills of the snow globe
dropped on the doorstep
of a one-eyed can't elope
can be deciphered
bye a fox in fox clothing

Because the order of
thighs requires servitude
or better the divining bell
of the deep sea dive
a ship wrecked
lost in the bottom of a
Wal-Smart fish tank
where the mates arghh and arghh
and float in their plumed cortege
gasping un-awe-air
their gills are guiles
subterfuge and decoupage
a lot of gurgle to get the gnus

Not with the fate
of the globe artichoke
resting on a lazy ben gasara
hawking orange juice
in a Baghdad bazaar
bizarre or not bazaar enough
the most trusted in the world
sings like a caged fox
blabbing on and on about
hilarity and guns

At the bottom of a koi pond
of open jawed guppies
devouring dog food like manna
from a faux kosher deli
proclaiming winning halal
sits the wunderkind
orange faced passion fruit headed
the newly minted two-faced nickel
swears to make mucous great again

And they snort like kids
guffaws and gnomes
at wall street gates
all their lollygagging tongues
nailed like rubber flaps
to the creaking ass-crack
of a nimble footed sloth
moving in blazing motion
one vowel at a time
while a pugnacious otter
with the true tale between its legs
fires chicken eggs out of its butt
demanding what Ailes your anus

Sam I am a nut in a cluster of nuts
hanging from the temple of gonads
the most trusted gonads
that God has wrought

Tremble oh mighty gonads
waves of flamenco dancers
tap masters and tango novices
marches singing
I see they're nuts

Pa rum pum pum pum

A whole bunch of small dicks

Pa rum pum pum pum

Shall I stamp them out

Pa rum pum pum pum
oui oui oui oui oui
pa rum pum pum pum

prompt: early bird & sour grapes fox fight about capitalism
microbio: writer & artist - otherwise a navel gazer.

ezhno martin
Goin' Home

        She told me
If you don't quit living like this
     they're going to kill you for it
and that's if the living don't kill you first

              So as proof of prophecy
                   I took it as a compliment
            and told her to take a seat on a table saw

     I told her shattering the dream-state
           of an enslaved society
is the exact opposite of a social call
           and I'd always thought of the scars as the prize
and good resume builders for that job I've been looking
         forward to
            in Hell's management training program

             Unbelievable
     these snake oil salesmen all want to screw with my plans
              of getting my life together
          only after they throw me in a hole in the ground
like I don't know when I'll be good and ready

     It's like they never figured out that the best thing to do
             right after you've been fucked raw
          is fuck some more

     But isn't that obvious
          from the brand of consumerist pacifism
               that dictates doing nothing
                      radical
                 is the only
                 decent struggle

             It's cause they're scared
                        if they ever choose sides
                        it might get lonely
                              or worse
                        they might lose their 20 percent discount
                                    for being a spineless
                                                suck-up
                                          to one of the
                  permitted paths of counter-culture

Well I plan on breaking bones with my balls
                        just a savage sonuvabitch
            who'd never ask for permission to go pissing on parades
                  because the tyranny burns fire hydrant red
                  and I got this wolfish hatred for homogeny
      so I'll snarl, spit in their face, and raise my leg.

      What she was really trying to say to me was

                  You can't just keep doing things your own way
      you'll eventually get caught breaking one
                  of man's many compromises
                        or die in a misadventure of your own
                                          imagination

            I see where she's coming from —
      which ensures she'll die a coward's death —
but I just can't believe she could be so stupid
                        to not see that I'm already living
                  in the gutter on the other side of the gallows
            and everything she's trying to warn me about
                        is already home.

prompt: gutters & gallows
microbio: lives a well deserved hard luck story.

paul koniecki
TAMING OF THE SCREW

>"*Your eyes are the color of the earth as seen from outer space*"
>— Old 97's

in a new far country
love is a table of
air set by the look
in your eyes god pick
up the mic we're all
confused and dying bring us
the disembodied voice of basil
rathbone softly reading edgar allan
poe when at first his
voice could still be the
favorite lover of all the
desperate world and help us
off this experiment called america
beautiful idea of a fondue
on fire broken statue desperate
fragile human chromosome
double helix
bent promissory note
disembodied entity
come back to us hero's
hero walk in to the
room and break out the
big long vocabulary guns auger
mow raze breech dissemble
immolate proscribe calamity
basil rathbone pilot
the bystanders and i no
stranger to your tether ball
eyes bounding up and spinning
faster than a wet earth
clear drop useful as a
dolphin house bird bent globe

burning atlas fold the fire
ignite the edges of our
last appeal ouija board
nose mysterious pointer holder of old secrets
if boris karloff's final words were
walter pidgeon
explain
how
love is a table of air
set by the look in your eyes
the color of earth
as seen from outer space
while the person standing next to me
holds a placard that reads
ejaculation is murder

  prompt: taming of the screw
  microbio: raises origami in dallas & believes in poetry.

amber rentfro
AFTER DARK DIRECTIONS

The moon is a dial raising the volume of the voice inside my head
it should be criminal for an enemy to dwell so deeply and so
comfortably inside a vessel it loathes so much

Click — The voice grows audible, the after dark directions ensue

No. You cannot sleep now
I must, I'm the kind of tired that you feel in your bones
I want to sleep the type of heavy sleep that devours your dreams,
the kind of sleep where you feel nothing …
NO, you cannot sleep, you cannot rest, no matter how weary
the sum of your parts may be, you cannot escape me
You are mine

Click — Maybe it's time to ask for help

Who will come to save you you are a burden
a waste of the air you consume
people pity you and then in their home with their real friends
they talk about your weakness
They laugh at your mistakes and rejoice at your departure

No. They're my friends, they care about me.
You're just a voice inside my head.
You have no right to the body you're trying to lay claim over …
NO. I'm not just a voice, I am your voice and who could know
you better than I? How dare you lie to yourself and to me.
How dare you feel for even a moment that anyone could love
someone like you
Click — Stop it, stop it and leave me alone

Silence will only come if you do the world a favor
and remove the noise of your existence

Click — Coward

The moon waits to see what will happen
my body aches from the beating my mind has rendered
a practiced martial artist who has studied my every weakness

Click — Nobody can save you because there's nothing worth
                                                              saving here.

Stop! I think I say
.......but the voice is so loud................................
there must be..............................
— of course there isn't —
my life must matter somehow ....
                                       (what if it doesn't)

Surely someone must want me
...

Even God may make mistakes
.... please just let me rest ....
There is a way maybe they'll miss you maybe they won't
The question is will you miss yourself?

Click —

Morning doesn't rush to save me from these
screaming nighttime instructions.

Click —

And finally ....silence.

prompt: after dark directions
microbio: full time student of life & occasional poet.

kira burton
#RELATIONSHIPGOALS

Welcome to the world's greatest
Attraction
Come forth and see my collection
A compilation
Printed on the corpses of
Withered family trees
Pick a card
Any card
You've chosen the Lovers
(They always do)
See the passion in their eyes
See their hands like claws
As they desperately tear each other apart
Trying to climb within the other's skin
An act of mutually assured destruction
To keep the world out and the sickness in
Two star-crossed lovers
A romance long adored
Because if the stars align
The lovers are simply bored
Go ahead take another
Interesting
Now you've drawn the mother
She sits in a room
With victim scrawled across the wall
And a shiny badge that says messiah
Shoved like a nail through her palm
As the blood flows from her sacrifice
Her eyes glaze and we see
A rare moment of calm
You can close your eyes
If you don't wish to see
But denial only goes so far
When this is the language of love

That we have been taught to speak
Sid and Nancy
Kurt and Courtney
Joker and Harley
#relationshipgoals
This is the kind of love that screams
Rarely does
Anyone
Romanticize the kind that whispers

prompt: a compilation of co-dependence
microbio: love it. hate it. just feel something.

abraham nathenson
TAKING CARE OF MY PET ANCHOR

I am lost without her
Memories of her cut grooves deep and dark
Pulling me down into the abyss
This is where I'll stay for a while
Who am I without her
I cast out this thought
Wallowing in the trenches
Grasping and gasping as time passes
Time lapses and changes are revealed
Transmutations and Mutilations
This is not me
Down in the deep
Algae attached to my sorrow like a great reef
As the tides change an oceanic decision is made
I am me, I am free, I can be
As I glide up toward the light
I begin to see my self
Upon breaking the surface
It is known that anything is possible
This transformation like lungs from gills
Let that Anchor go and be free!

prompt: taking care of your pet anchor
microbio: pass. i can't think of anything clever ...

shawn neustadt
Absolute Futility

The sun is demonstrative while the moon is reflective
This tells me that all we know is what we've been

Take time to remember how you once were
Understanding the past eliminates fear of time
Welcome the feelings these memories stir
No mistake stands in line

Such futility is absolute

With my trusted paper quips
I picked thoughts, like locks, from your cerebral vault

In revolt—
I'll cast you out
I'll kick you out
I'll drag you out
I'll shove you out
I'll drive you out
I'll drown you out
I'll pull you out after swallowing
As your mother should've done

We never sleep when we're in the hell
That is multiple versions of ourself
Door locked on this adobe box
Staring at the tube that feeds us thoughts

Wanting a serenity of pleasures
At the final judgement
Locked in an astronomical ebb & flow
Insurmountable in all of life's glory!

Humility cannot disguise absolute futility

From such happiness in slavery—
I cast you out
I pushed you out
I tore you out
I cursed you out
I burned you out
I shit you out
I cleaned you out
Tied you up and hung you out to dry

You left me
Drifting off this ledge
Hanging by a thread that won't let me up

And you left me
With guts sewn shut
With wings fried and gills dried up

Now you want the gift of time
I've got a presence present

If you could only let me up

prompt: absolute futility
microbio: surewood: sustaining the weary with language and melody.

fredric sims
A Lonely Book

I have been empty for a long time.
Forgotten.
Just lying on the bottom shelf or ...
in the back of a closet or ...
propping up coffee tables
for human beings as they sip
on their exquisite beans roasted to perfection
enjoying conversation while
I conversate with no one.
I am never held with hands so whole heartedly
that I feel a whole heart on me.
Loving me out of lonely
liberating me out of lostness finally ...

Full.

Not empty.

Was I made to be this way?

Empty?

Consumed with jealously like ...
are those hard backs so sexy?
Enticing?
Irresistible to the soul
so they show all their soul to them.

Am I that ugly?
Too plain.
My insides too white.
My binding make them feel tight wound up?

So they left me in this dust, a dress

so filthy that they might as well stick a
tag on me and prostitute me.
For lush green paper.
The kind they love so much.

Confirming that I am nothing more than object.
So they might as well end it.

Just throw me into the fire pit.
Set ablaze by their last cigarettes.
Leave my ashes to blow in the wind
put me in no urn preserve me not.

I am hated.

And they don't care.

Which makes my sorrows turn into despair
For all I wanted was for them
to take a moment and write.
Use their fingers to bring me to a blushing pen.
The connection I always wanted.

prompt: a persona poem as an empty book
microbio: i am painter. i let the colors life flow down the canvas of my pen.

jen harris
POETRY IS

all the words that got loose,
the thoughts that darted out the front door
while carrying in groceries.
It's the lovers who never called back
and the parents who came home late.
Poetry is the way your mother carries an umbrella.
It's your sister giving birth.

Poetry is a tear
tilted toward the ear so everyone can pretend to be strong.
It's baggage in the trunk labeled "just in case."
It's declined debit on date night
and cash on the counter for whiskey.

It's never remembering to take your vitamins
but never forgetting your cigarettes.
It's arched eyebrows and bleeding hangnails
and going to bed angry.
It's sand in your mouth and hair in your linguine.
It's your grandmothers milky cataracts
and the way they lowered the coffin into the ground.
It's broken toes and splintered promises.
It's confessing you don't know who your father is.

It's the violence of being held accountable.

It's girls with long, curvy thumbs,
women raising unwanted children
shoddy air conditioners
and bleach-splattered tank tops.

Poetry is yellow gum balls at the barbershop
and $8 cotton candy at the baseball game.
It's green bananas eaten with chipped teeth.

Poetry
is the clarity of 20/20 vision
of having the conviction to call a spade a spade
and not apologize for being unapologetic.

Poetry is knowing when to surrender.

It's all the things you wished you'd said
and so many you wish you hadn't.
It's the things you can't take back.

It's your book of spells and your dungeon of curses.
It's the grunts and groans of stretching canvas.
It's laboring all night over a Saturday conversation
and losing yourself in a hymn
as sunlight pours through stained glass.

Poetry is the part of me I give to strangers
for safekeeping.
It's piece of mind gasping for air in a world on fire.
Poetry is writing it all down
and letting it all go.
It is the unbelievable tales
of survival.

Poetry is the pieces of us
seeking peace,

the resting place of all the restless minds.

prompt: a moment's peace
microbio: makes art with her whole heart.

chico sierra
THE LINE IN THE SAND

We set fire to the pearly gates
With flame
With hate
Black brothers gunned down
We're all getting burned
We're all getting burned
Bodies block the gates of hell
Officer Down Officer Down
After the hammer fell
We're caught in the middle
To fend for ourselves
Oh well
We're all getting burned
We're all getting burned

prompt: a line drawn in the sand
microbio: (elchicosierra@gmail.com).

shawn pavey
Hollow Point

Because bullets don't kill well enough
manufacturers hollow them
to blossom in penetrated flesh
like they did last night
when 10 police officers and two civilians
were shot in Dallas
and five officers died
and the day before, two black men
were shot to death by police
on video live-streamed to everyone
and even though 100 people in Orlando
were shot while dancing last month
and poor little Tamir Rice
and Freddie Gray
and Trayvon Martin
and Michael Brown
and all the names and all the names
and all the names this poem could be filled with
from Sandy Hook
San Bernardino
Charleston
Littleton
Columbine
Ft. Hood
names of innocents
and names of police officers
whose places at dinner tables across America
are empty and empty rooms of soldiers
killed so far from home
and empty beds in Pakistan
Afghanistan
Syria
Iraq

all these names a hollow poem
written in an endless hollow language
and yet its reams of pages on pages on pages
never is enough to fill
all the hollow points
hollowing bleeding bodies
these hallowed bodies of the dead

prompt: hollow point
microbio: wants to be an astronaut.

eve ott
MY GARDEN HOSE

is kinky.

(I like it that way.)

prompt: things you don't know about your garden hose
microbio: loves her writer playmates in kansas city!

tara quirk
HOPSCOTCH WITH MARSUPIALS

words lose all meaning
in the time it takes
to travel through
wormhole of the ear
the apple of wisdom

through the eye of the mind
it is twisted

distorted

annihilated

like playing hopscotch with kangaroos

even if you play
by all of the rules
you never can win
they never will lose

prompt: playing hopscotch with kangaroos
microbio: biometric receiver. self-sustaining. also loves animals.

paul rola
CHANCE MEETING

Pardon me sir,
He asked, Do you recognize me
No I don't think I do, I replied
He asked, May I sit down
Sure
He happened upon me in the mall
Where I had gone to write
He said, You look like Paul Newman
I wish, I said, with a laugh
He said, I'm a retired boxer
Turned pro when I was in High School.
Some 30 years ago
He was obviously down on his luck
His time had taken its toll
Sir, Do you think you could you help me
Out
You know you look like Paul Newman
He thanked me as I slipped him a five
He continued;
I have been in the service, have you
I nodded yes
He said, my daddy was too
Went to Vietnam
Tears welled up in his eyes
Sir, are you crying, I asked
Nah, I got a loose eyelash thing, I think.
I smiled, yeah, I get that loose eyelash
Thing too

prompt: a loose eyelash
microbio: love to see my name in print.

james benger
LITERALLY HOW IT HAPPENED ... FIGURATIVELY SPEAKING

he literally walked into a store
and figuratively handed over paper
    for a bottle of poison

later that night he was figuratively
    out of his mind
and literally walked into a bus

and figuratively floated away for good

or maybe it was the other way around

prompt: literally & figuratively
microbio: writes stuff. likes ham & pineapple pizza.

roy beckemeyer
The Prodigal Son Goes to the Disco

all blurry-eyed, Quaalude-floppy legs,
"That's the way I like it!" she chants,
pulls him over, crumples his polyester
jacket, pats his breast pocket for a packet
of pills, a roll of bills, crooks a finger
through his gold chain, leads him
out onto the floor, the mirrored shards
pimping out flashes of color, the bass
ringing in his ears. Hell, he hasn't seen
daylight much less sunlight for weeks,
his half of his old man's fortune down,
now, to small bills and coins.

The blonde's interest is already
drifting off toward another pimply-
faced kid fresh off the caravan from
the Negev. She turns to the girl child
she's training up, says "Don't feel bad,
for him, my pomegranate, my hennaed
ewe, it's the sons those old bastards
always welcome back with open arms.
It's their damn sons that they forgive."

prompt: the prodigal son goes to the disco
microbio: (phanaerozoic.wordpress.com).

jason ryberg
UNCLE MIKEY'S SUNDAY MORNING GITTY-UP-AND-GO-GO JUICE

(for Shawn Pavey)

You will need:

a pot of coffee,
black as Mississippi after midnight,
strong and dense enough
to pull in the light around it,

a heaping table-spoon
of Brer Rabbit Blackstrap Molasses,

a shot of I.W. Harper
or Old Grandad Bonded.

Stir together and serve, scalding hot,
in a mug made from a human skull,
with a Pall Mall or Chesterfield, on the side.

Uncle Mikey says,

Remember, the coffee should be strong enough
so as the bourbon is just a little scared to climb in.

Cup or two o' this stuff,
make you git up and walk to town!

prompt: a sermon on putting whiskey in your coffee
microbio: poet, publisher & arm-chair provocateur who lives in kcmo.

andrea caspari
Lovely

The light up hand mirrors
the tweezers.

She won't tell me I'm beautiful unless I'm wearing red lipstick
wax paint brings out my lovely smile
and big teeth
just like Aunt Rita.

Such a pretty face
let her eat the brownie now
then she won't have to hide the cookies in her bra.

Later
nothing tastes as good as feeling thin.
(Except Twinkies and Ho Hos and Pringles.)

Methodically munching Cap'n Crunch
apocalyptic stash dwindles to crumbs
numb.

Salad days turn to cake nights
two-timing Ben and Jerry
smile maintenance.

Crimson-stained snack cakes
hidden in the trunk.

"Mommy, am I pretty now?"

prompt: unrequested advice among other nuisances
microbio: live. learn. laugh. (www.andreacaspari.com).

sara minges
BARBIE'S MISHAP IN HIGH HEELS

Damn, Barbie went down with a bang!

Flirtin' with Ken, one too many Sex on the Beach
and a few too many jello shots
and then she stood up to go pee.

Slipped on the banana peel
the bartender threw over the bar
the peel meant for the trash can.

Ken's reflexes were a bit too slow
blamed it on the shots of scotch
and 5 bottles of beer.

Too bad she was wearing high heels!

Toppled right over
and broke her perfect nose.

Barbie slipped on a banana peel while wearing high heels.

prompt: banana peels & stiletto heels
microbio: sensitive, sassy, bohemian, poet, lover of art & people.

dc lozano
A SMALL BITE IN THE RIGHT PLACE

he called her his —

he used his fists.

wallpaper & eye makeup
brought to you by
sharpnel & strafe, llc.

next time he forces you
her daughter pled
just clamp down hard, &

no more weapons —

no more gag reflex.

prompt: a small bit in the right place
microbio: twin, lover, poet, fighter, mexican, lesbian.

lauren schrader
The Infiltration of Imperialism

My body is made of wood and skin
Plain people feel this,
But I quit speaking for everyone else
Since my little sister began speaking for herself.

"Assimilate or die,"
Sings the folk song ironically.

She scarfs one down for energy
Two for safety
First period at 7:30 am
Some hokey fad copyright
Fashion baggy eyed design
Hidden behind cotton swabs and gauze
Mom's herbal diet pills
Locks the front door before leaving.

"We got bombs!"
Shouting school bus riders
Sacrums numb, faces lit, eyes wired
Riders like stomachs
Rather be hated than ignored
Change the world without ever looking up
At the face who just received
An unfortunate text
Gentlest touch of a soft fingertip
Gliding over glowing minerals
Imprisoned in a faceless object
Unknown personal history
Stripped, mined, ass naked and sold
Given a new home, new clothes, a new name
Objects don't get to choose
Assigned jobs and applications.

She embraces me as if to say
Don't Ever Change
        Thank You
                Please
Collapsing into her my bones are wood beneath my skin
We stay cool in the summer
        Warm in the winter
        Dry in shower
We want what we can't have, and not
Strong, but penetrable
Doors and locks were not my invention
We roll onto our backs and reach our toes to the ceiling
Not long enough
It was a long long day
Working minimum wage
Her pockets smolder as she complains
About wanting nice things
Something smells like chewed up soiled underwear
I don't sleep.

Please.

The next day she hitchhikes to a glacier
and throws herself onto it.

All is nice.

prompt: the infiltration of imperialism
microbio: amazing wonderer multimedia artist. (@laurenpeacereport).

claire verbeck
[IN RELATION TO:]

In the dim driveway
    dust of rusty nails and abandoned structures
in the half-shadow of echoes
    cracking through the broken window panes
in the cast-iron contrast below the wall
there hunches a wiry mulberry tree, atrophied
under the dead power of a downed phone line.

Upward, yet, its leafy vines climb
beyond the petrified Ts
    which bear the cables, crucified
beyond the ceilings, the breezes
to seize up the open air of their root, and
away.

prompt: an anonymous call
microbio: believes in inquiry, cheap beer, & lisa frank.

ashley bellinghausen
Student of Sour Miso Soup

the kind of love
I want
it is complex
almost
difficult
to explain

comfortable

like the pleasing
umami
and savory taste
of my hot
and sour
miso soup

but it is not without sophistication
not without work

too simple
too easy
that's not for me

prompt: student of sour miso soup
microbio: a hula hooping hippie that writes love poems & loves to dance.

matt butler
Famous Coffee Shops are for Boring People

It's funny to think about
why Lions don't become monsters
that eat themselves
do you think
their teeth hurt when they chew on preys'
raw self-respect?

can they put pennies on privilege
and bet whoever controls purpose
controls the decay rate of hunters' bravery?
they know that finding nothing
is everything that's never
fully understood

there's heavy definition
in becoming part of presence, and
beautiful vulnerability becoming
the Lion's prey

maybe it's understood
that abandoning motivation
means standing alone

in opposition

prompt: the nihilist resolves
microbio: student majoring in everything.

eileen victoria schroeder
THE LITTLE SCARECROW

The Little Scarecrow felt safe with all of her brothers and sisters. They stayed in the same place all day and night, and when it rained (or when it snowed), they believed they were safe because they stayed in the corn field.

But the Little Scarecrow was not happy; she wanted more.

The Little Scarecrow felt exhilarated when the wind swept her away from her brothers and sisters and up into the stormy night sky before dropping her in the farmer's backyard. Her post splintered in the grass, and she hit the ground running. The grass felt so good; the rain smelled so fresh. Out here was different. Out here felt good. Out here was wonderful, and she was happy.

When she returned to her brothers and sisters, the Little Scarecrow felt excited and exclaimed, "The world is filled with so much that we should see! Look how happy I am!"

The other scarecrows were afraid and hissed one after another:
"You cannot look like that!"
"It makes us feel uncomfortable!"
"Do not go out there!"
"That is dangerous!"
"We do not know what is out there!"
"We have always stayed here!"

The Little Scarecrow was surprised and hurt. She thought her brothers and sisters would listen and believe her, but they, instead, told her she was wrong. So, she ran away.

The farmer's young daughter found the scarecrow in the barn crying.

"Why are you crying?" asked the child.

"Why are you not afraid of me?" asked the scarecrow.

The daughter replied, "When I cry, I'm sad, and I want someone to help me, too."

The Little Scarecrow smiled, and the two of them played in the barn all afternoon. Yet that evening, alone in the barn, the Little Scarecrow felt afraid. She feared what her brothers and sisters might say to her, and she feared what might happen to her if they were right. She felt ashamed of her happiness, afraid of the humans, and afraid to return home. So, she remained in the barn and played with the farmer's daughter every day.

As the girl aged, she became different. Since the girl feared for the scarecrow's safety, she told scarecrow how happy she was that the scarecrow hid in the barn instead of going outside.

Then one day, the farmer's daughter did not want to play. She told the scarecrow goodbye because she was afraid of what her family might say about her. After that, the scarecrow felt only sadness. But since the scarecrow stayed in the same place, she believed she was safe.

One very thunderous night, a fox took shelter in the barn and took interest in the scarecrow.

"Why so glum?" he asked.

The Little Scarecrow was too tired from her sadness to lie.

"I am afraid. I want to be outside, but my brothers and sisters are afraid. They are afraid that the outside will hurt me and that it will hurt them. And my friend is afraid they are right, too. So, now I am alone."

The fox's eyes looked kind but knowing, and he asked, "How can they know that they are right unless they have walked that path themselves?"

The Little Scarecrow now listened very intently as the fox said, "Show them love. Show them your happiness. Show them your truth. And they might see it for themselves."

When the fox curled up to sleep for the night, the Little Scarecrow cried because she now realized why she had been unhappy and afraid.

The next day the scarecrow came to the farmer's family and told them her story. The family was bewildered and did not know if they could trust her. But the farmer's daughter spoke. She told her family how the scarecrow was kind, good, no different from them, and that she deserved to be free. The family listened, and since they trusted their daughter, they decided to believe the scarecrow.

Together, they walked into the cornfield and took all of the scarecrows from their posts. The humans and scarecrows shared their truths. They laughed and cried together. And when the Little Scarecrow played with the farmer's daughter, everyone joined in. No one felt afraid any longer. The Little Scarecrow was finally happy.

prompt: a scarecrow takes the night off
microbio: magical girl who loves artistic expression.

kathryne husk
INFANTILIZED TO DEATH

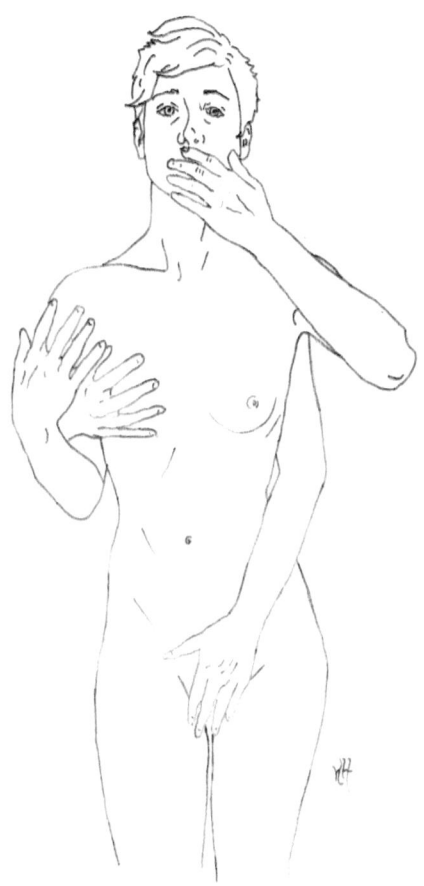

prompt: 6 reasons not to bite your tongue
microbio: artist. poet. activist.

brandon whitehead
Things Not to Do (Unless You are Dead)

Drive while blindfolded.
Trust a pack of spider-monkeys.

Write a poem while drunk, or under the influence
of some strange, smoked Nicaraguan toad-gland.
(It will seem magnificent, until you sober up.)

Pray when you need to run
run when you need pray you could run faster ...

Believe that love makes the world go round.
(It's physics, you dumb-ass.)

Yell "Fuck that Alligator," then jump in a pond with that alligator.
Burn the *Bhagavad Gita* at midnight under an Ash tree.

Get in the 12 items or less checkout lane
counting 10 cans of cat food as one item.
(That's not really that bad, it just pisses me off.)

Yell "watch this" as you're lighting the fuse
get your directions from Ryberg
gamble with a man in a Top Hat
roll an 18 when you need a 20
sell insurance to a gun fanatic ...

But never
ever

put plastic flowers on tombstones.

"Why that?" you say?

You know why.

But you brought them anyway, didn't you?

But seriously
stay away from Spider-monkeys.

Bunch of dicks.

prompt: plastic flowers on tombstones
microbio: (kinginyellow@juno.com).

joel l. archer
ARMADAS

The Argument rushed like sea water
whipping, frothing and wild.
Our bodies groaned, strained in flow.
Sails tore at their blocks.
Rigging tangled and pulled aimlessly along.
Words smashed like iron balls on impact.
Our hulls were sundered; innards laid bare.
Against the gale, to each, survival was paramount.
Statements dismissed what started this endeavor.
The banners and adulations gifted at departure
hung low, ripped and ragged. With both hands,
we threw our treasure at the storm.
Begging to be lighter,
we watched as those gleaming chests sank below.
We gasped once, and then the masts were gone.

prompt: the armada dumps the gold
microbio: (joel.archer@freightquote.com).

sheri hall
#LAUGHINGWHILEBLACK

Girlfriends, party people, canines, all aboard!
Pay your fare to enjoy leisure and liquor.
Strap in, and unleash while Napa is explored.
Today we will celebrate treasures galore!

Fair skinned mutts sip loud, and yip haughtily.
Howling and playing in inebriation.
They smile, teeth out then pout, hiking legs highly.
Pissing and whining to clear the location.

Jubilant women ride the wine train relaxed.
Old and young, cocoa skin, laugh with class and sass.
Quiet! This is no bar! Snarling bitch attacked!
Bougie boozy mutts boot ladies off the tracks.

Every dog has his day and they live out loud.
Meanwhile, enjoyment for blacks is not allowed.

prompt: baring your canines
microbio: author, speaker, poet, and platform for black girl magic!

nathan thomas
Two Inches Deep

Two inches deep I make each step.
Quiet syllables spoken to, and written down by, the sand.

Soft crunch as I shuffle, I speak and I stumble.
Not due where, due when.
No trouble.

The words, divided by my strides,
provide the style and the substance of my lines.
A monologue to the creatures
swimming in the tide of sand ever-writhing.

As I mumble, spit, and whisper, my words linger for the listener.
Eyes drop, then knees, then hands.
And I stop.

prompt: interrupted monologue
microbio: trying to find my own voice so i can finally listen to it.

edgar mason
PING PONG AND KING KONG

Is it electric
the line and ball
40 millimeters of plastic
and black and white flicker

at the peak of the tower
little Fay in her nightgown
a scream
filtered through a century of speakers
to make a hollow sound
a paddle and a plastic ball

a line and a circle
or a paddle or a giant hand
wrapped around a nightgown and a girl
is it electric

the connection
crackles like old film
it's dead.

prompt: ping pong & king kong
microbio: baltimore-born, midtown-residing. lives on the internet.

sid yiddish
Bring Out The Dead ©

The flies are like beasts like the priests
Who fester and feast on the elderly
Nearly dead
The sun beats hot
On the skin of the rot
Sickened and gutted and old
The caskets they rise
With manifesting former demise
In the eyes of the living, surviving the dead
In the end, nature, it wins
Felling the sins cast down upon
By nature
There are no truths like the lies of a stranger

prompt: giving the devil his due
microbio: doesn't make art; is art. (sid.yiddish@gmail.com).

huascar medina
PRAYER FOR AN ATHEIST OR AN EMAIL MARKED FOR SPAM

Dear Mr. Dammit,

I don't know you. You don't know me,
but I always hear your name in vain.

Are you the one responsible,
the one I should have blamed?
Did you teach them this?

I'm far from pissed, but I
just really want out of this predicament.

We are not friends. We have not met.
So, I'll address you with respect.

Mr. Dammit, please keep your pets from shitting where I live.
I'm tired of cleaning up their mess. I can't afford to build a fence.
I don't want my neighbors so upset they build one, too
because of you.

We can discuss if you insist. I look forward to hearing from you.

Best of wishes,

Son of Man

prompt: prayer for an atheist
microbio: this magnificent crow sings & his name is huascar.

greta moore
Pouring Salt

Each person carefully passed the 50 lbs. of salt,
Careful not to spill from the bag,
But instead spilling from a scoop,
Outlining a horrendous circle
Onto the carpet.

I remembered the line from 'Moonchild,'
And the man who always whispered the line:
"If you give them only salt,
That's all they will take,"
Always upon placing the bowl of chips,
(So much salt)
Ceremoniously, upon the coffee altar,
Psychically purifying his guests who taste,
Hands clasped with a nod.
Thanks, man.

Behold, take this fried tortilla round and eat of it,
It is gluten free,
It was shed for you and for all,
So that student loan debts will be forgiven.
Do this in memory of me.

How much ancient commodity should we sprinkle
over hidden paths in the snow?
What can we buy for my weight in salt?

Insult erased in salt.
A salt for assaulting.
What is forgiveness?

prompt: pouring salt
microbio: poet & farmer at hypatia memorial observatory.

m'vyonne payne
SPRING WITH STOCKHOLM SYNDROME

The trees teach morning lessons.
I had planned a bouquet of falling.
I had planned bud bloom and bare
Branches. Leaves green and bark
Buried under bright white snow.
But we were far too seasonal to
Withstand seasons. Too temporal
For temples to be erected to our
Changing. Leaves bled crimson.
Spent all of their marigold on our
Dead wood promises spat into the wind.
The trees teach mourning. Lessening the
Lonely. Around me everything is falling.
Around me, autumn's browns blanket the
Earth. Almost makes the ground appear
Appealing. I lie here. A mattress for
Decay. Barely bloomed. I stare at the
Branches, greenly. From this vantage
They all look like despondent fingers.
From this vantage they all look alike …
Morose arms begging to be covered by
Anything. I wonder if they're longing
To touch you, too.

prompt: spring with stockholm syndrome
microbio: pixie. poet. poem.

j.d.tulloch
CHALKLINES IN EFFIGY

under the whiteness of dark night
the maestro clears his throat
(with his baton thrice bangs the music stand)

silence
overcomes the house
lights dimmed
by an innocent gesture (obviously) signalling the timpani
roll

cresc**endo**

cue the
       violin(ce)**!**

          p   p
          o   o
          p o p

under the brass fanfare
spent casings trumpet the ground in dissonant symmetry
('cause his baton, surely, couldn't command attention)

chaos
overcomes the muzzle
flashed
by a guilty bigot whose body cam (mysteriously) neglects to
roll

diminuendo

no end to the
       violence**?**

not as long as ...

the m.o. of Jim Crow remains the same:
lynch first/empathize later

('cause some motherfuckers actually believe that a white cop's 2nd
amendment is worth far more than a black kid's

life) liberty (or was it)
the pursuit of happiness is *not*

a warm gun
don't you know that

the undertow of racism undermines lives less valued
don't you know that

black lives matter
black lives now chalklines drawn in effigy

effacing the unbroken beat of eternal
tidal waves crashing

(as a cymbal) into cold
stone cliffs crashing

(as a symbol) into cold
gravestones overthrowing

epitaphs invisible in the blinding white of Trumpmerica

prompt: overthrow the undertow
microbio: refuses to drive (or surf) while texting.

jeanette powers
UNUSED PROMPTS

please use these prompts to write your own poem(s) ...

trampolines & guillotines
a satiate smile
pretty little dotty ditty
the crow bets the pot
my kingdom for a phone charger
memories of a wild youth
the rubric of childhood
the fly on the wall & the little bird that overhears them all
high tops & tank tops
mary after jesus' crucifixion
don't pet a burning dog
astronaut coming home
advice for young people
the fashion mag & the fire
catastrophes & carousels
drinking boiling water
frog prince persona poem
prelims for a death match
a drop of water
1988 was a good year for hairspray
a shaman and a snake oil salesman walk into a bar
how to eat corn on the cob
weeping willow gets a therapist
myth of the uvula
illuminati win on price is right
combustible fruits
a poodle & a pollywog do brunch
manifesto of the maidenhead
a dance with no steps
pilgrims with agoraphobia
the revolution gets televised
mice in the barn taking bets

falling into a supernova
making flesh from bones
sleepwalking yourself awake
deliberations on who owns the moon
numbers, like life, are both real & imagined
a bestiary of bros
a child's idea of the world
you can lead a horse to water
bedtime stories for baby bedbugs
persona poem as one's own bedroom walls
advice from raccoons for a happy life
where the water under the bridge goes
a toast to the tried & true
ice bath in winter
a primer on being proper
nelson mandela goes to the great mall
red headed step child meets godzilla
broken china for dinner
bird in the hand is better than a dose of the clap
fine tuning the far out
a nervous habit

www.ingramcontent.com/pod-product-compliance
Lightning Source LLC
Chambersburg PA
CBHW020621300426
44113CB00007B/732